E
JAC   Jackson, Ellen B.

Ants can't dance

DUE DATE **BRODART** 08/92 12.95		
OCT. 1 9 1992		
NOV. 3 0 1992		
FEB. 0 8 1993		
MAR. 1 5 1993	MAY 26 93	
MAR. 2 2 1993		
APR. 1 2 1993		
MAY 0 3 1993		
MAY 2 6 1993		
OCT. 1 9 1993		
OCT. 2 5 1993		
MAR 2 9 XIV		

Ants
Can't
Dance

by **Ellen Jackson**

illustrated by **Frank Remkiewicz**

Macmillan Publishing Company   New York

Collier Macmillan Canada   Toronto

Maxwell Macmillan International Publishing Group
New York   Oxford   Singapore   Sydney

To my mother
— E. J.

For Frank and Clara
— F. R.

There was once a little boy named Jonathan whose parents knew many things. They knew how to paint doors and how to do chores. Jonathan's father knew about caterpillars and cheese. Jonathan's mother knew about oatmeal and bees. Between the two of them they knew almost everything.

Jonathan didn't know everything yet, but he was learning. Every day he went to school and learned a little more.

One day Jonathan was walking home from school when he saw a strange sight. An ant was not walking in the usual way.

Oh no! It was skipping and tripping as sassy as could be.
Jonathan got down on his hands and knees to see what was
what. The ant was tap-dancing. Tappety-tap-tap. Hop, hop, hop.

Quick as a blink, Jonathan scooped up the ant and raced home to show his mother and father.

"Mother. Dad. Come look. I found an ant that can dance," said Jonathan.

"Now, Jonathan," said Jonathan's mother. "Ants can't dance."

"Absolutely, positively not," said Jonathan's father.

"This one can," said Jonathan.

He put the ant on the table.

"Dance, little ant," said Jonathan.

The ant just stood there and looked at its toes.

"Maybe some music would help," said Jonathan. He put on a record of "Tea for Two." The ant walked over to a bread crumb and started munching.

"Jonathan," said his mother. "Ants can't dance."

"Not even the jitterbug," said Jonathan's dad.

Munch, munch went the ant.

"Well, it's *my* ant and I'm
going to keep it, anyway,"
said Jonathan. He scooped up
the ant and put it in a glass
jar with some bread crumbs.
Then he carried the glass jar
to his room.

Tappety-tap-tap danced the
ant as soon as they were
alone together.

The next day Jonathan was walking home from school as usual. He was very busy thinking about his dancing ant. Suddenly he heard a voice say: "Pssst. Over here."

Jonathan looked around, but no one was in sight. Then he noticed a peanut lying on the sidewalk in front of him. He got down on his hands and knees to look the peanut in the eye.

"Pass the salt and butter the corn," said the peanut.

"A talking peanut!" said Jonathan. "Wait until Mother and Dad see this."

Quick as a blink, he scooped up the peanut and ran home to show his parents.

"Mother. Dad. Come look. I found a talking peanut," said Jonathan.

"Oh, Jonathan," said his mother. "Peanuts can't talk."

"Absolutely, positively not," said Jonathan's father.

"This one can," said Jonathan.

He put the peanut on the table.

"Talk, little peanut," said Jonathan.

The peanut just sat there doing nothing in particular.

"Jonathan," said his mother. "Peanuts can't talk."

"Not a word," said Jonathan's father.

"Well, I'm going to keep this peanut, anyway," said Jonathan. "It *can* talk when it wants to."

He carried the peanut to his room and laid it on the windowsill. Tappety-tap-tap went the ant in the jar, all six ant feet doing a quick shuffle.

"Higgledy-piggledy, pigs in a pile," said the talking peanut.

"Drat you, peanut!" said Jonathan. "Why wouldn't you talk for my mother and father?"

"I'm shy," said the peanut. "And a little nutty."

The next day Jonathan was walking home from school again, thinking very hard about his dancing ant and his talking peanut. Suddenly he heard whistling: "Tweedle dee dee. Diddle diddle dee dee."

Jonathan looked around, but no one was in sight except a tiny stone lying in the middle of the sidewalk. Jonathan got down on his hands and knees to see what was what.

''She'll be coming 'round the mountain when she comes . . .'' whistled the stone.

''A whistling stone!'' said Jonathan. ''Well, I don't suppose it will whistle for Mother and Dad, but I'll take it home, anyway.''

Quick as a blink, he scooped up the stone and ran home.

"Hello, Jonathan," said Jonathan's father. "How was your day at school?"

"Did anything interesting happen?" asked Jonathan's mother.

"Not a thing," said Jonathan.

"Oh say can you see . . ." whistled the stone from Jonathan's pocket.

"What was that?" asked Jonathan's father.

Jonathan pulled out the whistling stone. It was still whistling "The Star-Spangled Banner."

"Why this is amazing!" said Jonathan's father.

"A whistling stone!" said Jonathan's mother. "We must call the museum at once!"

Soon, Jonathan's house was full of important people. A famous geologist had come to examine the stone. Newspaper reporters were talking to Jonathan's mother and father.

The stone whistled, "Over the river and through the wood to grandfather's house we go . . ." as loud as a piccolo.

At last the geologist was ready to make her report.

"This is a very rare stone," she said to the reporters. "We must take this stone to the museum and study it at once."

"But it's *my* stone!" said Jonathan. "I want to keep it."

"A stone like this belongs to the world," said the geologist, scooping up the stone and putting it in her bag.

The next evening Jonathan's parents read all about the stone in the newspaper. It was being studied by many important scientists. After that it would appear on "The Tonight Show" whistling with a rock group called The Rolling Stones. It had even signed a contract to make movies in Hollywood.

"And to think, we discovered it," said Jonathan's mother.

"But it's *gone*," said Jonathan. "It doesn't belong to me anymore."

"It's a very famous stone now," said Jonathan's father. "You wouldn't want to stand in its way, would you?"

"I suppose not," said Jonathan.

"This stone business has made me think twice about your ant and your peanut," said Jonathan's mother thoughtfully.

"Oh, Mother," said Jonathan. "The ant ran away yesterday, and I ate the peanut this morning."

"Martha, you know as well as I do that peanuts can't talk," said Jonathan's father.

"And ants can't dance," added Jonathan. "Good night."

He walked quickly to his room. Hidden in the back of his closet was the glass jar with the ant in it.

Tappety-tap-tap danced the ant, sassy as could be. Hop, hop, hop.

"Hoist the Jolly Roger," said the peanut. It was hidden in one of Jonathan's shoes.

Jonathan crawled into bed holding the glass jar in one hand and the peanut in the other hand. The ant was doing high kicks.

"Tell me a story," whispered Jonathan to the peanut.

"Once upon a time there were three bears . . ." began the peanut. But before it could say another word, Jonathan was fast asleep.

Printed and bound in Singapore   First Edition   10   9   8   7   6   5   4   3   2   1

The text of this book is set in 15 point Cushing Book. The illustrations are rendered in pencil and watercolor.

Library of Congress Cataloging-in-Publication Data · Jackson, Ellen B. Ants can't dance/by Ellen Jackson; illustrated by Frank Remkiewicz. — 1st ed.   p.   cm.   Summary: No one believes that Jonathan has an ant that dances, a peanut that talks, and a stone that whistles. ISBN 0-02-747661-8 [1. Humorous stories.] I. Remkiewicz, Frank, ill. II. Title. PZ7.J13247An   1991   [E] — dc20   90-5942   CIP   AC